PREFACE

Fundamental Studies for Timpani is a beginning method covering all the essential timpani techniques. The studies contained in this volume were designed to prepare the beginning student for performance of standard band and orchestral literature.

Fundamental Studies for Timpani is divided into three main sections. Section I contains technical studies incorporating rolls, cross sticking, muffling, and staccato strokes. Embellishments and dynamic changes have purposely been omitted in order to allow the student to concentrate on technical problems. Twenty miscellaneous studies which feature marks of expression, embellishments, musical terms, and a variety of time signatures comprise Section II. Section III contains twenty-four short tuning exercises which should thoroughly familiarize the student with the most common intervalic changes. These exercises may be used in conjunction with Section II.

For further study refer to:

Whaley, Garwood. **Musical Studies for the Intermediate Timpanist**. N.Y. JR Publications, Inc. 1972.

To

MEREDITH and GAR

SECTION I

PRELIMINARY STUDIES

HAND POSITION

Carefully observe the correct grip of the timpani stick in the photograph below. Make special note of the following:

1. The stick is held between the thumb and the first joint of the index finger.

2. The third finger is used to support the stick (the fourth finger may also be used depending upon the type of stroke).

3. The thumb should be on top of the stick so that the back of the hand faces outward.

4. Both hands are held exactly the same.

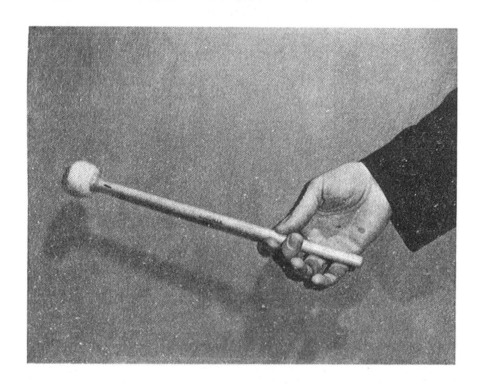

PLAYING POSITION

This photograph demonstrates the correct playing position. Carefully observe the following:

1. The elbows should be slightly curved so that the sticks form a V on the drum head. This will allow both sticks to strike the same playing area.

2. The sticks should be held several inches above the drums and parallel to the drum head.

3. Stand driectly behind both drums.

TIMPANI STICKS

A wide variety of sounds may be produced on timpani by the use of different types of sticks. Most professional timpanists use at least six different types. For the beginning student however, one to three pairs will suffice. The following types of sticks are suggested:

1. Medium felt head for general playing.

2. Hard felt head for staccato passages.

3. Soft felt head or cartwheel sticks for emphasizing tone and legato playing.

TUNING

Since the timpani are percussion instruments of definite pitch, it is essential for the timpanist to have a well-trained ear and be able to accurately tune the drums. The first step in achieving this goal is to develop the ear through singing exercises. To become familiar with the most important intervals, I suggest the following:

1. Learn to sing major, minor, and chromatic scales.

2. After accomplishing this, sing from the first note of a scale to any other note.
   The distance from one note to another is called an interval. The student's ability
   to recignize and sing intervals is absolutely essential. Below is a list of intervals
   as they occur in major and natural minor scales.

F Major

F Natural Minor

Many teachers use the method of associating familiar tunes with intervals to simplify memorization. Below are several examples:

Major 2nd: "Alouette"

Major 3rd: "Marines' Hymn"

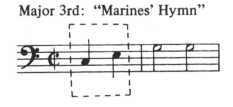

Perfect 4th: "Here Comes the Bride"

Perfect 5th: "Twinkle, Twinkle Little Star

Major 6th: "My Bonnie Lies Over the Ocean"

Use the following method when tuning the drums:

1. Sing the pitch to be tuned.

2. With the pedal depressed, strike the drum softly and step down on the pedal, stopping when the desired pitch is reached.

TIMPANI RANGE AND SIZE

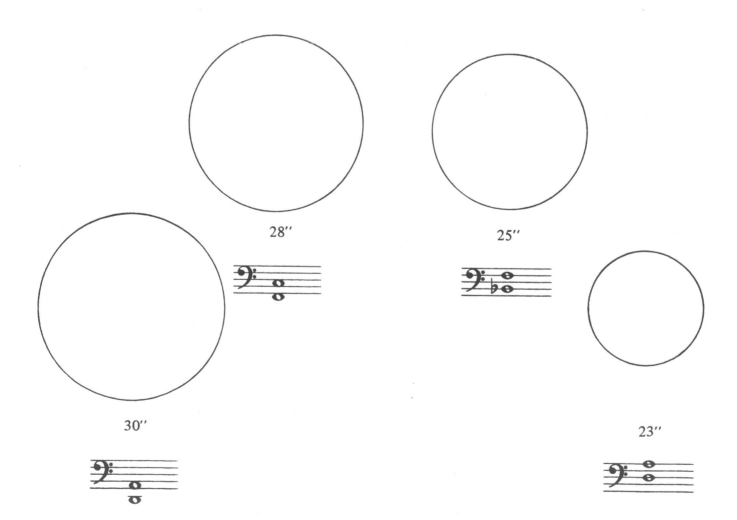

THE ROLL

The timpani roll is produced by alternating single strokes. The speed of the roll is determined by the size of the drum and the amount of tension placed on the drum head. A large drum with very little tension will require a much slower roll than will a small drum with a great deal of tension. Keep in mind that in order to produce a good roll, the head must vibrate at an even rate of speed.

Practice suggestions:

1. Hold the sticks loosely enough not to interfere with the natural rebound of each stroke.
2. Do not use hard ball staccato sticks for rolling except when absolutely necessary.
3. Be sure that both sticks strike the playing area of the drum head.
4. Practice rolling on drums tuned to various pitches.
5. Practice "attacking" a roll at different dynamic levels. Strive for an even sound through - out.

A–D

A-E

♩ = 104 – 120

24

MUFFLING

The technique of stopping or "dampening" head vibrations (sound) is called muffling. Muffling allows the timpanist to control the exact duration of each note.

Use the third, fourth, and fifth fingers to muffle. See photo.

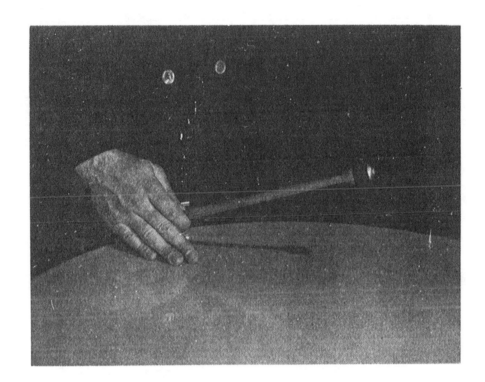

Practice suggestions:

1. Allow each note to sound for its exact duration, muffling only when indicated by a rest.
2. Do not "slap" the drum when muffling.
3. Pratice muffling using: a. the same hand that strikes the drum.
                          b the free hand.

28

THE STACCATO STROKE

Due to the low register of the timpani, it is often necessary to articulate certain rhythmic passages by using staccato strokes. This is especially true of rhythmic figures occuring below first space "A."

The basic staccato stroke is produced by increasing the tension between the index finger and the thumb and snapping the wrist. The intensity or volumn of this stroke is controlled by the amount of finger tension and wrist snap.

The following studies should be practiced pianissimo, using a"light" staccato stroke, and fortissimo, using a "heavy" staccato stroke.

F-C

CROSS STICKING

The purpose of cross sticking is to enable the timpanist to perform fast, rhythmic passages in a "clean," even manner. Use the photo below as a guide.

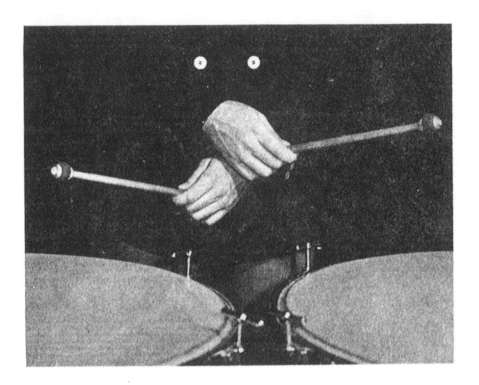

Practice suggestions:

1. Keep both hands close together and close to the drums.
2. Always strike the playing area of the head.
3. Be careful not to make a glancing stroke.
4. Usually passages requiring cross sticking are played using a staccato grip.

Practice the following basic cross sticking exercises (the X indicates the point at which one stick crosses the other).

34

SECTION II

MISCELLANEOUS STUDIES

The purpose of this section is to provide the student with studies which will develop musicianship and serve as examples of standard timpani parts.

The following studies combine previously learned techniques with marks of expression, a variety of time signatures, and musical terms.

Study each exercise carefully. Work tor pertection.

36   When playing two notes simultaneously, both drums must be struck at exactly the same time. Try to "pull" the tone out of each drum. Sempre means always (always mezzo forte).

In this study concentrate on achieving an even, unaccented sound. Each note should be full and resonant.

38 Again, strive for an even, unaccented sound. Do not confuse eighth note triplets with the rhythm ♪♫ . Although often counted alike, these rhythms are quite different.

The dynamic changes in this study happen suddenly and without warning (subito). Be careful to maintain dynamic levels once they have been established.

40   The dots beneath the note heads are staccato marks. Notes marked staccato
should be played in a short, detached manner. On timpani, the staccato effect is produced
by increasing the tension between the first finger and the thumb, and snapping the wrist.

It is often necessary to use staccato strokes in order to reinforce a rhythmic articulation. This is often the case when a rhythmic figure is written at a soft dynamic level and on a low pitch as in measure two.

42

This study should be played in a vigorous, staccato style. Use cross sticking to insure an even level of sound.

The time signature ¢ or 2/2 is quite common. Become familiar with this meter.
Be sure to observe muffling indications, especially the two measure rest.

44 For rhythmic precision, dotted notes should be sub-divided (count: 1 e & a). Be sure that both the dotted eighth note and the sixteenth note are played at the same dynamic level

The indication "cresc." is an abbreviation for the Italian word crescendo which means to gradually get louder. Become familiar with meters based on half notes ($\frac{2}{2}$, $\frac{3}{2}$, $\frac{4}{2}$).

The indication "dim." is an abbreviation for the Italian word diminuendo which means to gradually get softer. Remember to sub-divide dotted rhythms.

This study deals primarily with appogiaturas or grace notes. On timpani, grace notes must be played "open" so that all notes are distinguishable. Always try to bring out, or stress the main note (𝅘𝅥𝅯𝅘𝅥𝅮 𝅗𝅥).

Be careful not to alter the pulse when changing from even to uneven rhythmic groups. Before beginning this study, practice the following exercise using a metronome.

This exercise is a study of soft dynamic levels. By playing on the edge of the head it is possible to produce an extremely soft sound. Experiment to find the best all around playing area for soft dynamic levels.

A crescendo is often indicated:

Likewise, a dimuendo may be noted:

Keep the pulse steady throughout the changes of meter.

Accents must be played in relation to the dynamic level in which they occur.
Since this study is mezzo forte throughout, all accents must sound alike.

A dash placed beneath a note is an indication to hold the note for its full value (tenuto). Notice, that although written differently, the rhythms in bars ten and twelve sound the same.

Forte piano rolls are executed by first striking the drum forte, allowing the sound to decay to piano, and then beginning the piano roll. The beginning of the soft roll should not be perceivable. This is an important timpani effect and should be perfected.

The abbreviation SFZ stands for sforzando which means very strongly accented. Poco rit. means a slight holding back of the tempo.

A combination of elements from preceding studies is found in this exercise. Try to make the crescendi and diminuendo gradual and even. Poco a poco means little by little.

SECTION III

TUNING STUDIES

The following section contains a series of twenty-four short tuning exercises. These exercises will familiarize the student with various interval changes and aid in acquiring the ability to change pitch during a rest.

As a systematic approach to these exercises, I suggest the following:

1. Determine the interval between the fixed pitch and the desired pitch.
2. Using the fixed pitch as the root, sing the interval (desired pitch).
3. Release the pedal. Strike the drum softly stepping down on the pedal until the desired pitch is reached.
4. Be sure to count carefully while observing the above procedure.

58

60

G–C ♩ = 104

C to E
4

A–D ♩. = 104

D to B♭
4

G–C ♩ = 126

G to B
4

A–D ♩ = 116

A to F
4

G–C

G–C

G–C

G–C

62

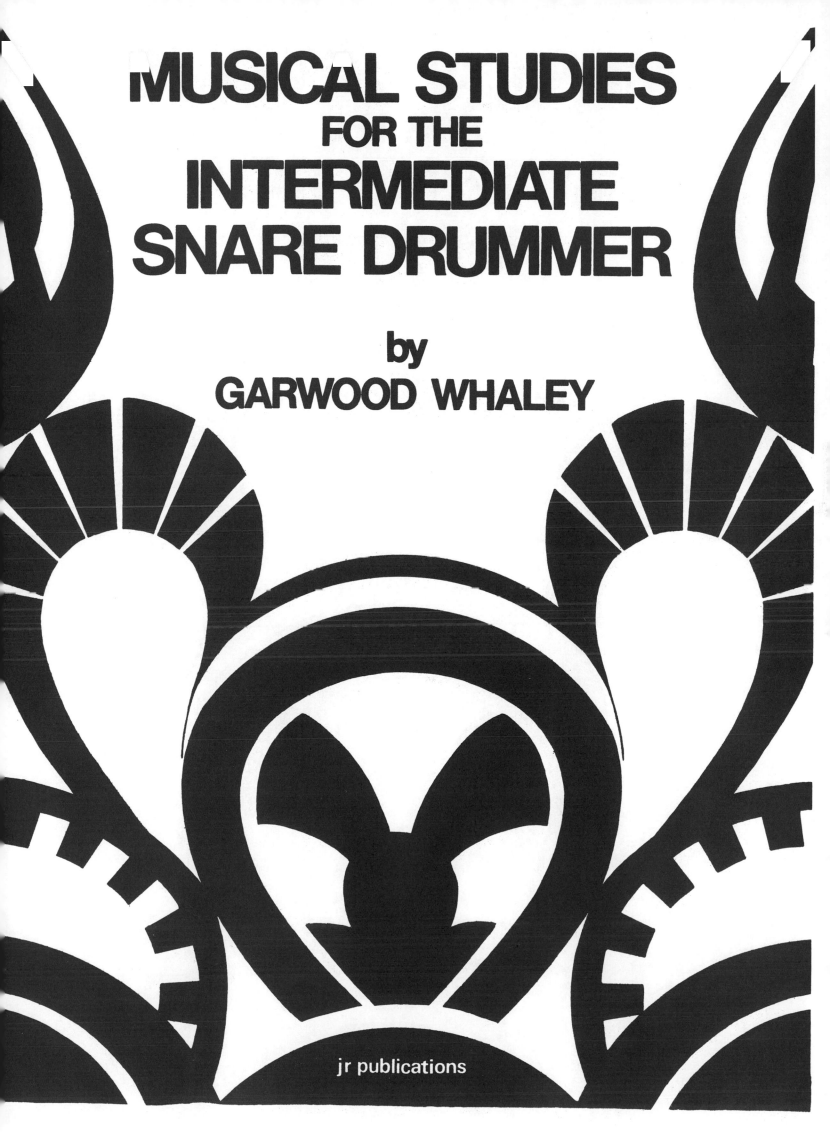

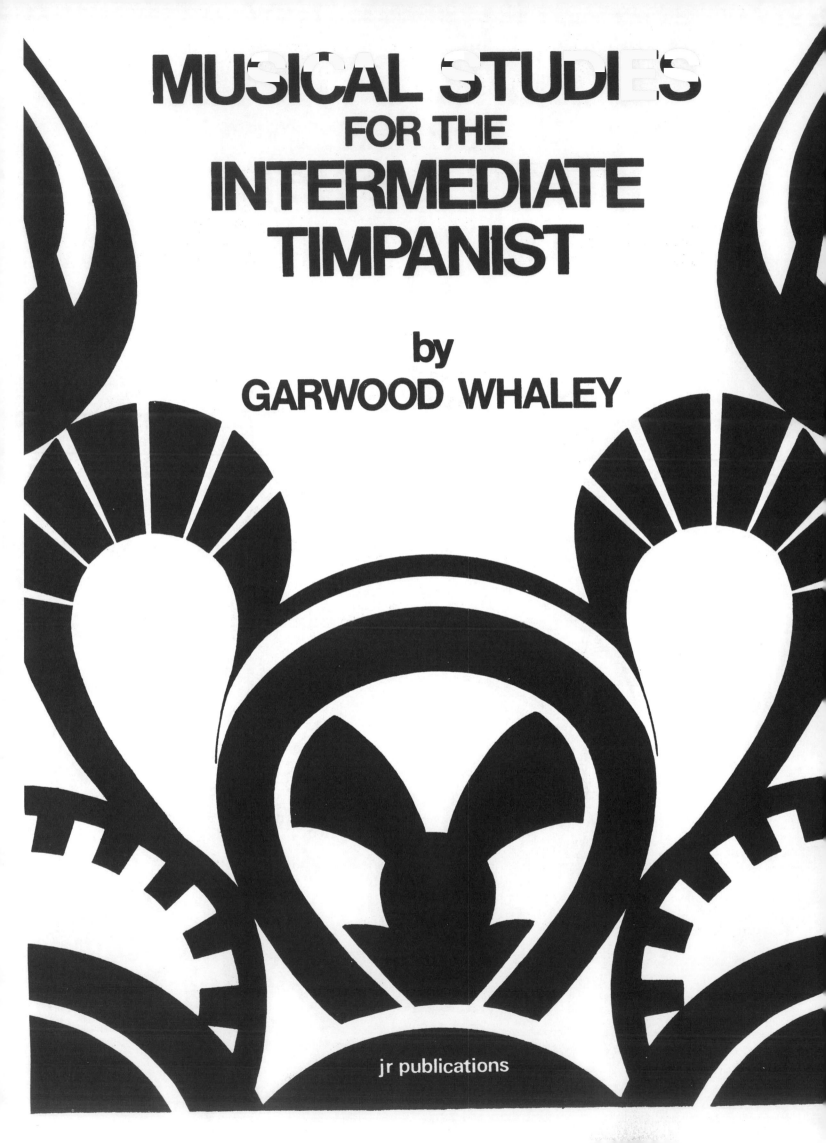